MW00803304

# Left-Handed Tenor Banjo Chords

by

**Mel Bay**

**Cover photo courtesy of Deering Banjo Company**

*Visit us on the Web at www.melbay.com — E-mail us at email@melbay.com*

# Index of Chords

# The Correct Way to Hold the Tenor Banjo

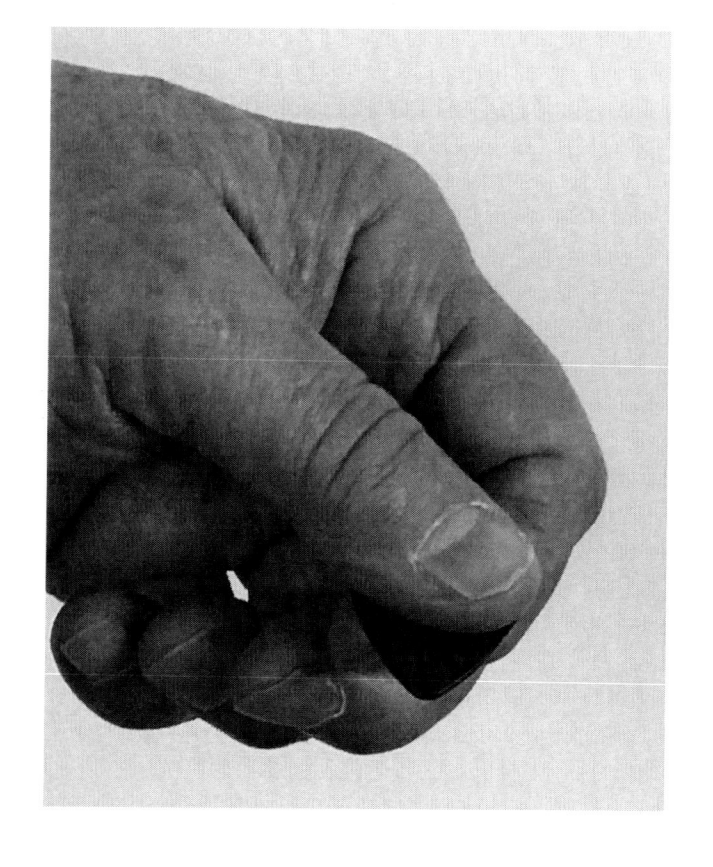

## This is the Pick

Hold it in this manner firmly between the thumb and first finger. Use a medium soft pick.

# The Right Hand

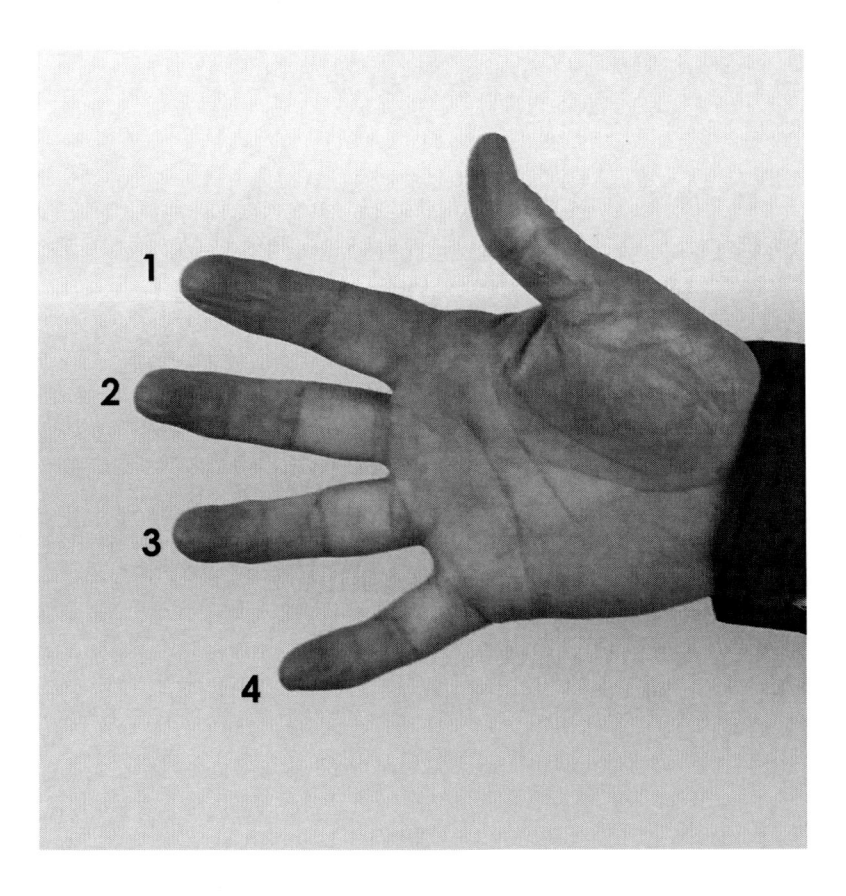

**Practice holding the tenor banjo in this manner.**
**Keep the palm of the hand away from the neck of the instrument.**

# The Fingerboard

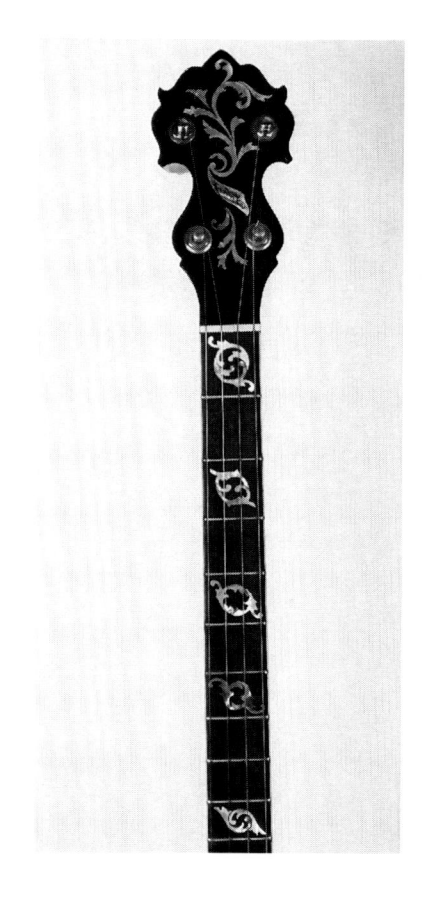

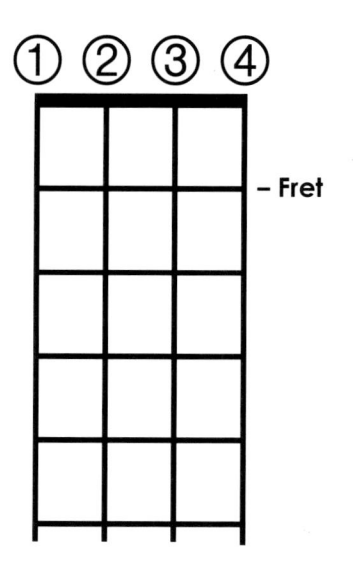

The vertical lines are the *strings*.

The horizontal lines are the *frets*.

The encircled numbers are the *number of the strings*.

# Striking the Strings

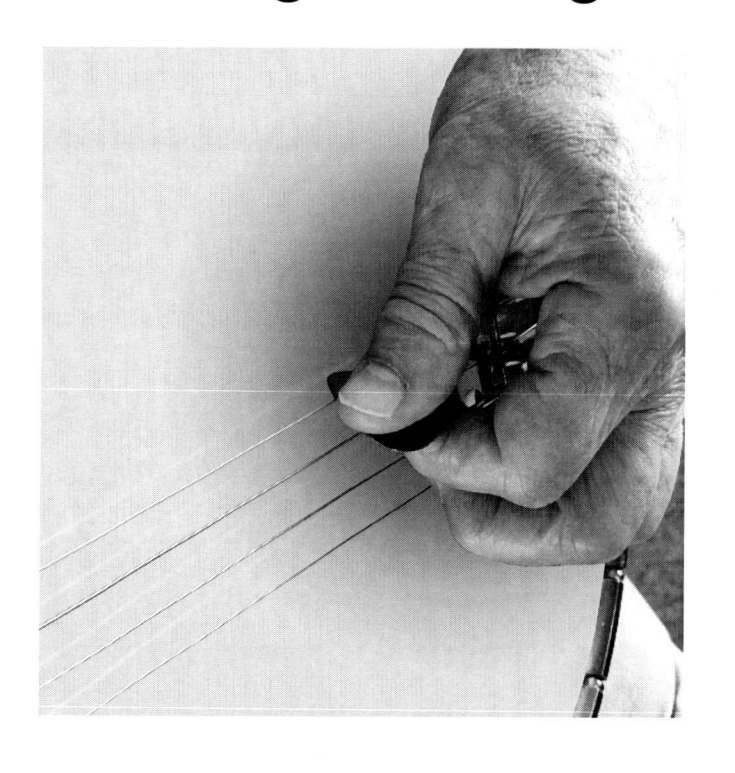

Downstroke of the pick.

# Tuning the Tenor Banjo

**A** ①    **First String**       **G** ③    **Third String**

**D** ②    **Second String**     **C** ④    **Fourth String**

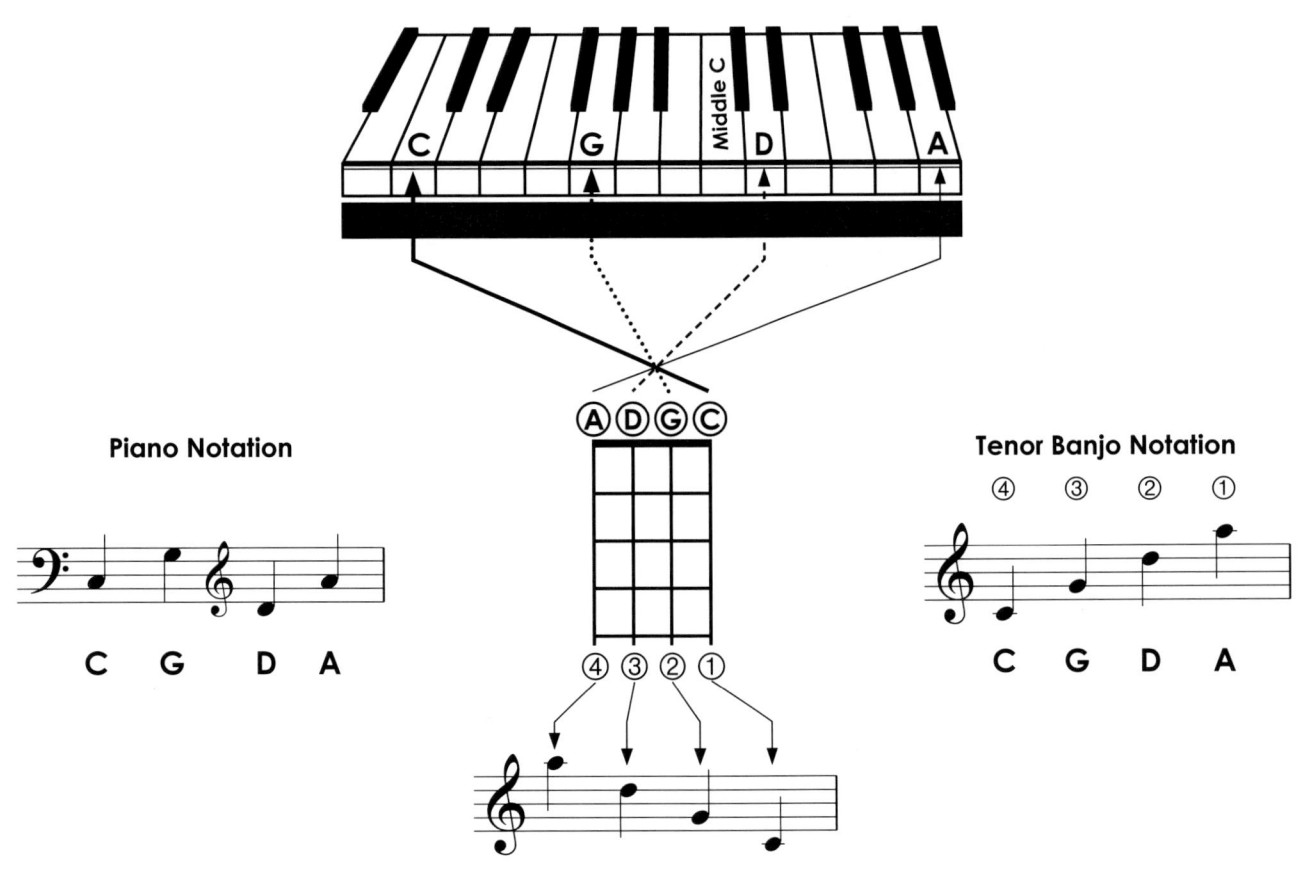

**Piano Notation**

C    G    D    A

**Tenor Banjo Notation**

④   ③   ②   ①

C    G    D    A

# Another Method of Tuning

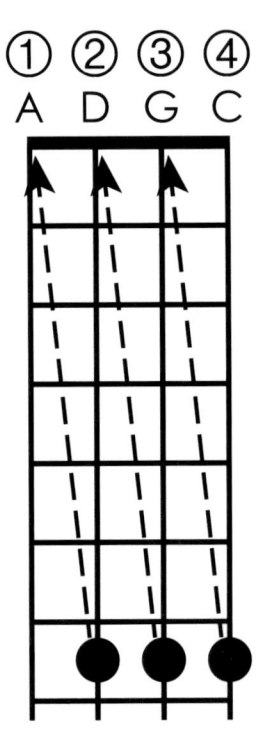

Place the finger behind the seventh fret of the fourth string to obtain the pitch of the third string (G).

Place the finger behind the seventh fret of the third string to obtain the pitch of the second string (D).

Place the finger behind the seventh fret of the second string to obtain the pitch of the first string (A).

## Electronic Tenor Banjo Tuner

Electronic tenor banjo tuners are available at your music store. They are a handy device and highly recommended.

# The Major Chords

**C**
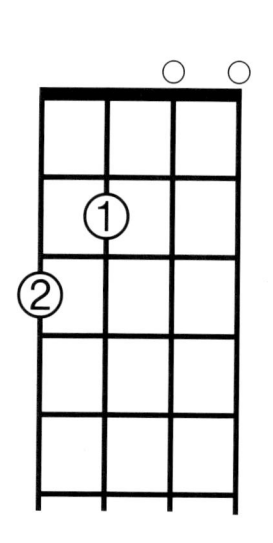

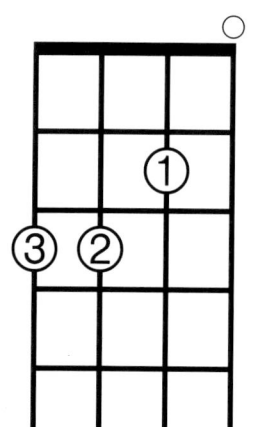
**F**

**G**

# The Major Chords

**D**

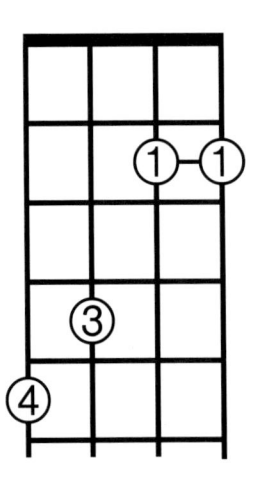

**A**

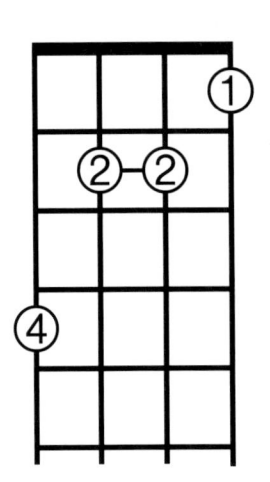

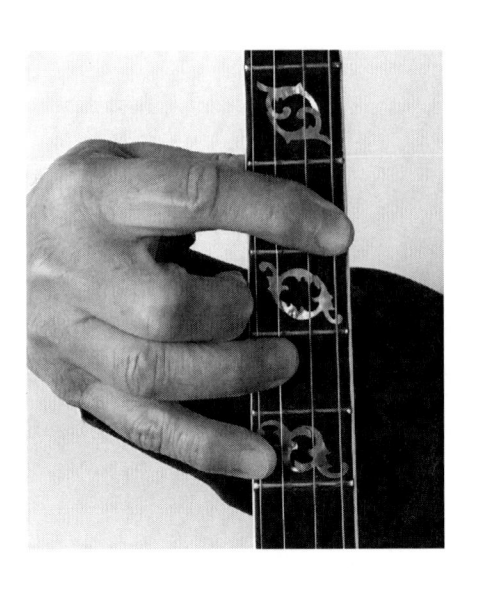

**E**

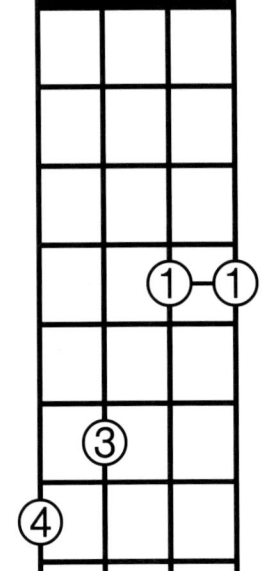

# The Major Chords

**B**♭

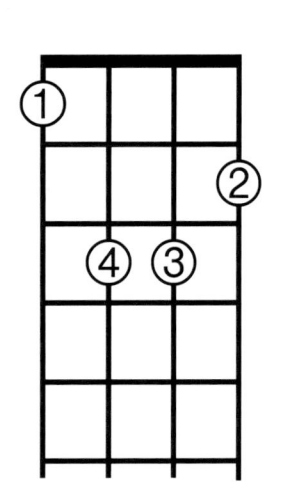

**E**♭

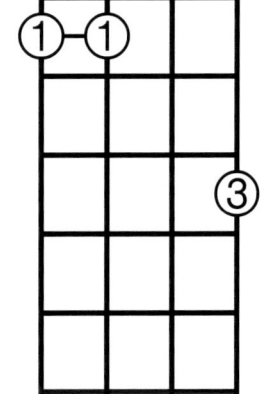

**A**♭

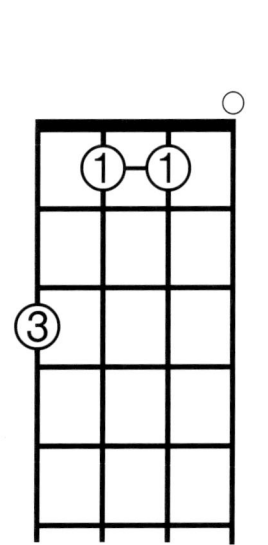

# The Major Chords

**D♭**

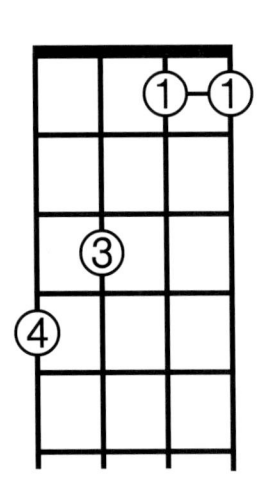

**G♭ or F♯**

**B**

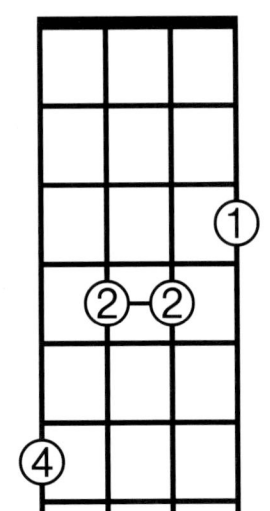

10

# The Minor Chords
## m = Minor

**Cm**

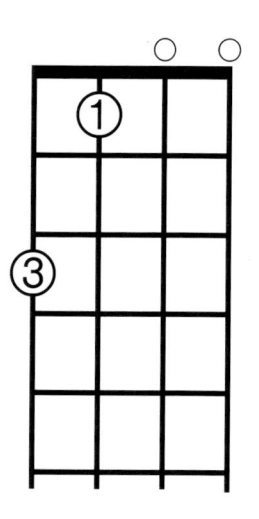

**Fm**

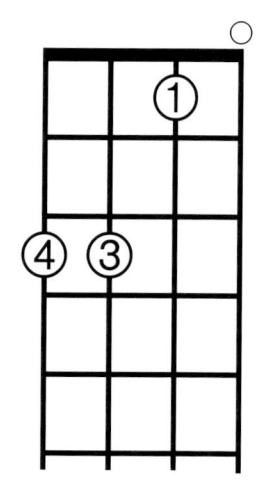

**Gm**

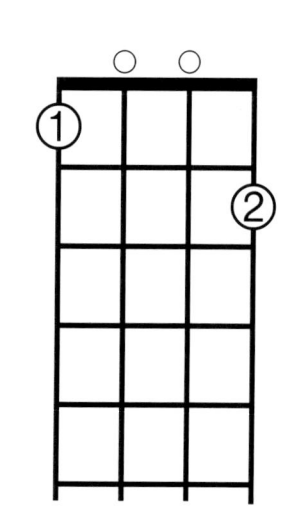

# The Minor Chords

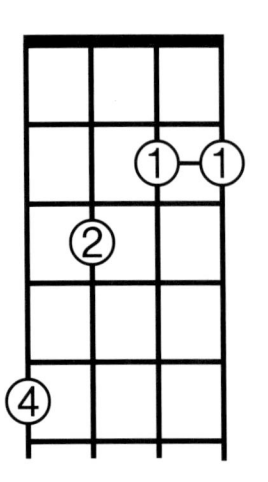

**Dm**

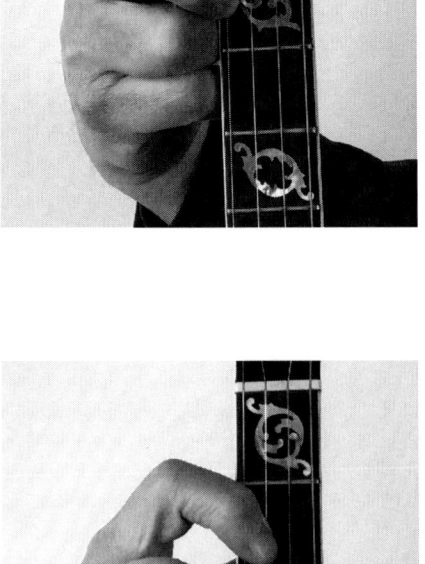
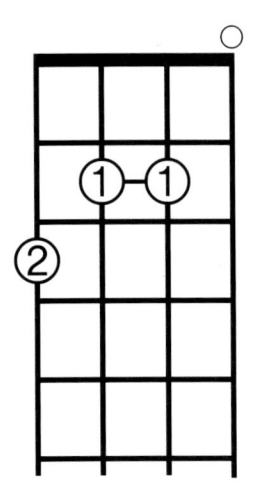

**Am**

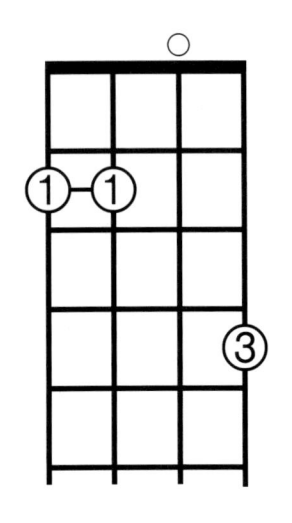

**Em**

# The Minor Chords

**B♭m**

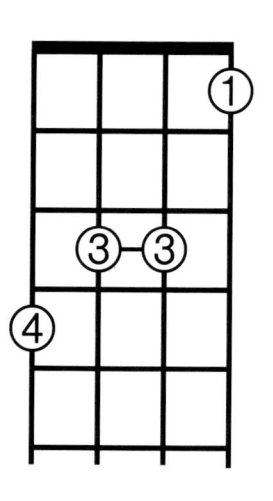

**E♭m**

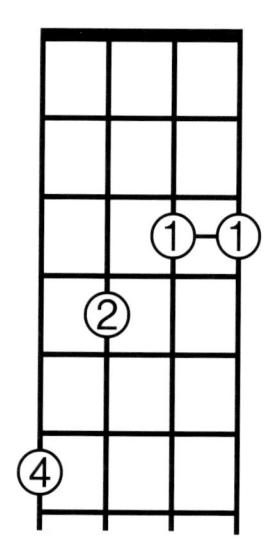

**A♭m**

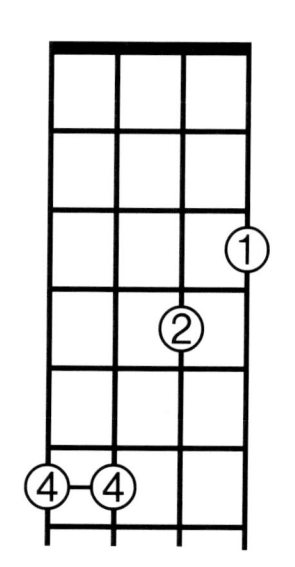

# The Minor Chords

**D♭m**

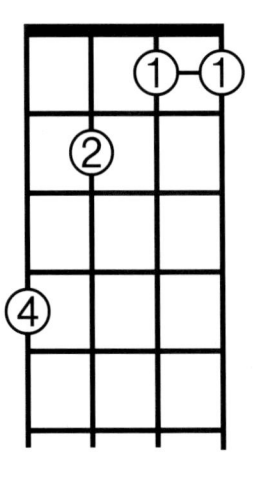

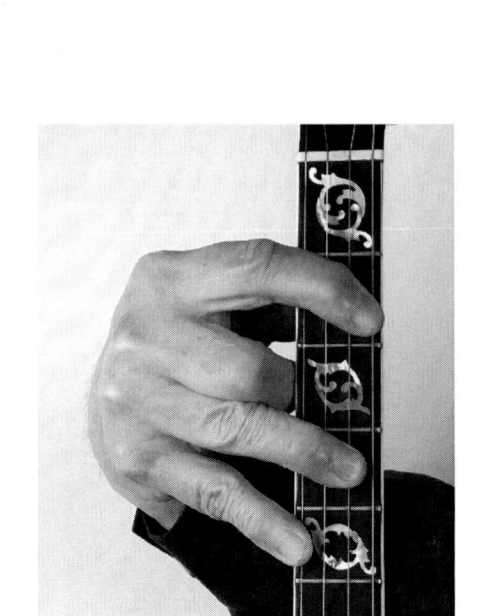

**G♭m or F♯m**

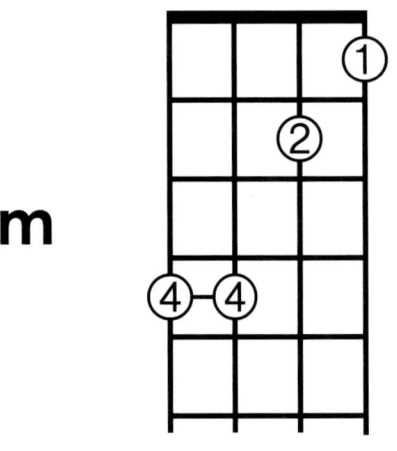

**Bm**

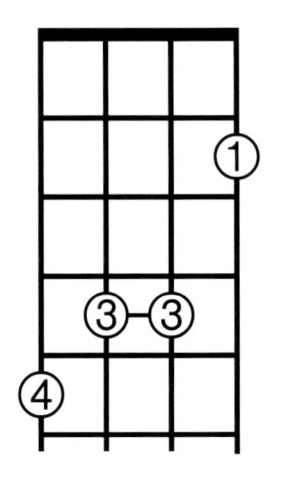

# The Seventh Chords
## 7 = Seventh

**C7**

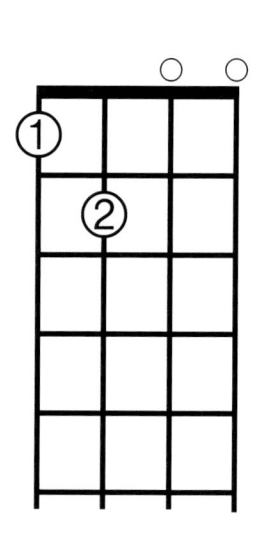

**F7**

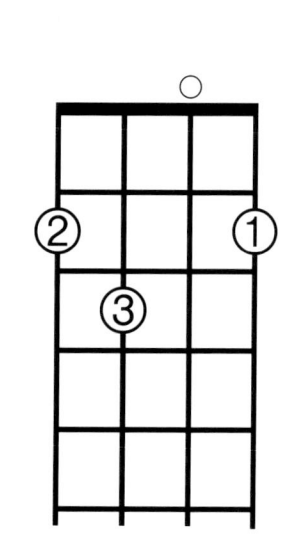

**G7**

# The Seventh Chords

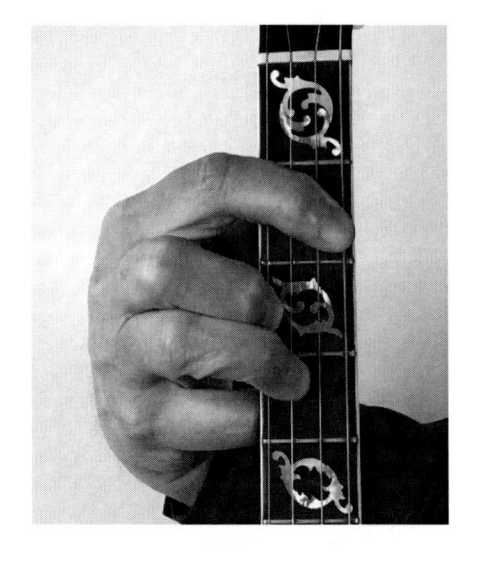

**D7**

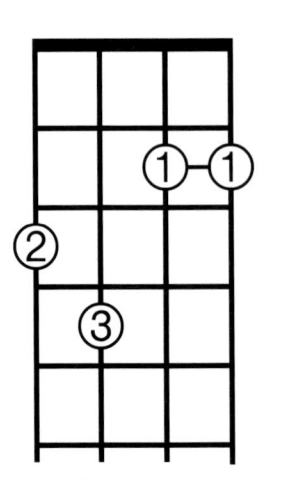

**A7**

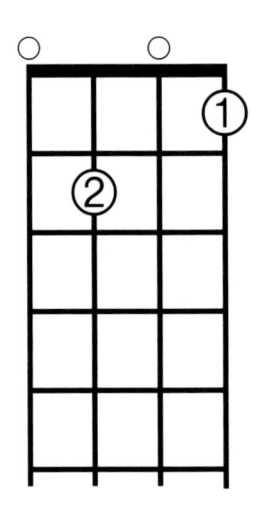

**E7**

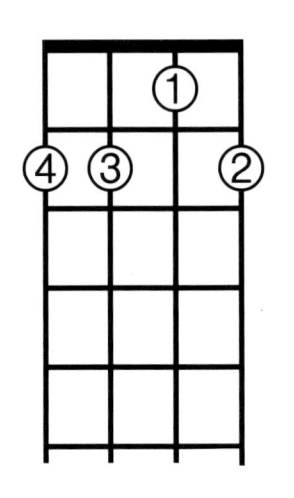

# The Seventh Chords

**B♭7**

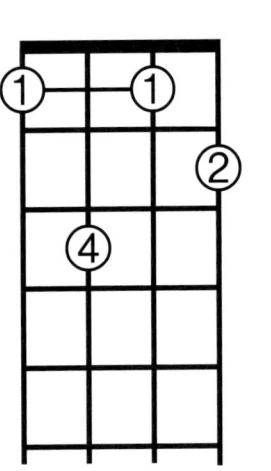

**E♭7**

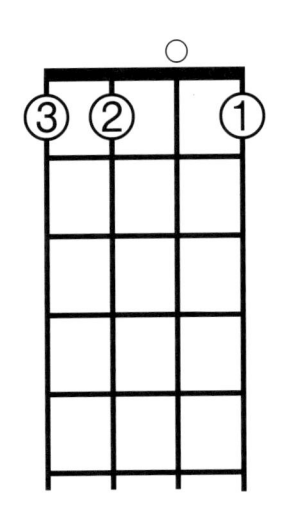

**A♭7**

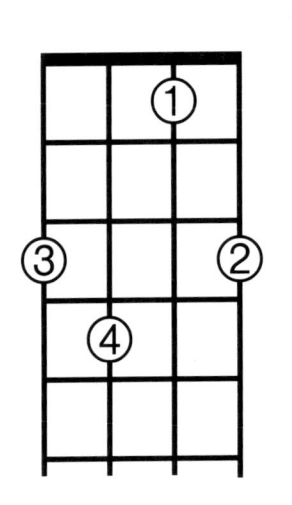

# The Seventh Chords

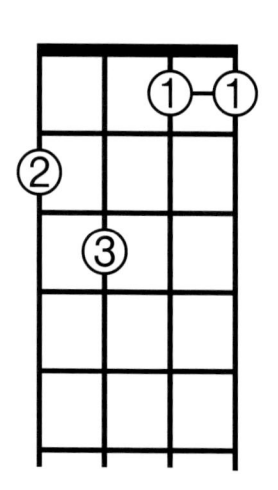

**D♭7**

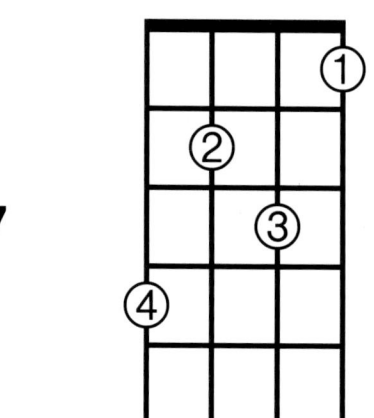

**G♭7 or F♯7**

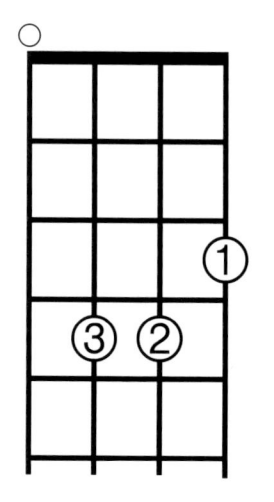

**B7**

# The Diminished Chords

## – = Diminished

Each diminished form can represent four different chords.

$\left(\begin{matrix}C\sharp- \\ D\flat-\end{matrix}\right)$ G– E– B♭–

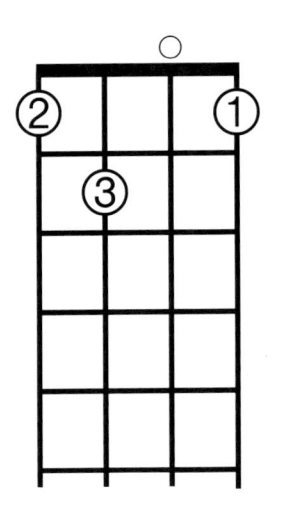

D– $\left(\begin{matrix}A\flat- \\ G\sharp-\end{matrix}\right)$ F– B–

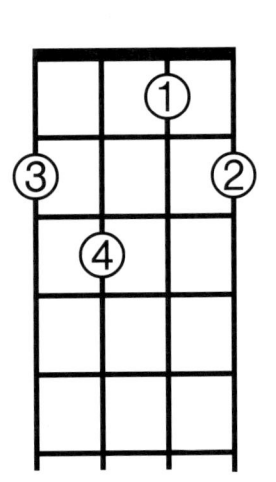

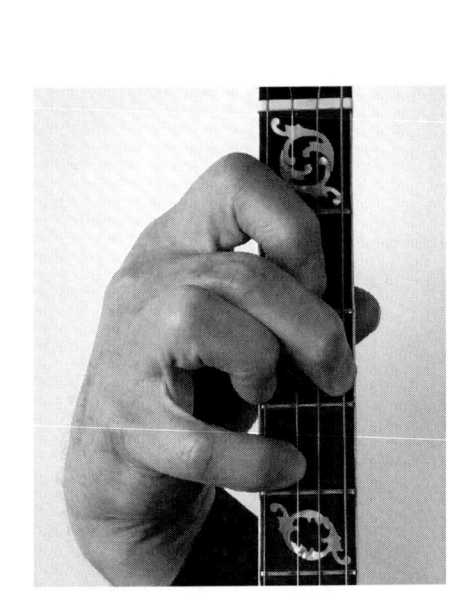

E♭– A– $\left(\begin{matrix}F\sharp- \\ G\flat-\end{matrix}\right)$ C–

# The Augmented Chords

## + = Augmented

### Each augmented form can represent three different chords.

 C+ E+ $\left(\begin{array}{c}\text{G}\sharp\text{+}\\ \text{A}\flat\text{+}\end{array}\right)$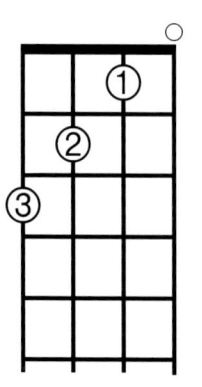

 $\left(\begin{array}{c}\text{C}\sharp\text{+}\\ \text{D}\flat\text{+}\end{array}\right)$ A+ F+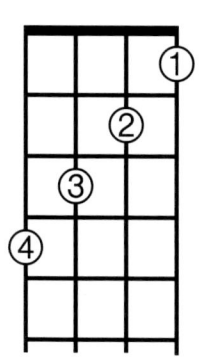

$\text{D+}\left(\begin{array}{c}\text{F}\sharp\text{+}\\ \text{G}\flat\text{+}\end{array}\right)\text{B}\flat\text{+}$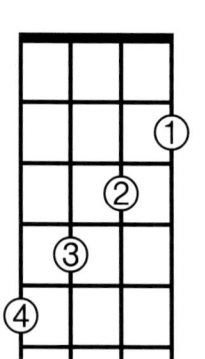

 E♭+ G+ B+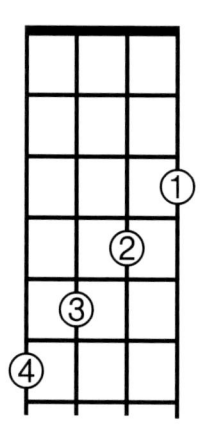

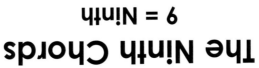

# The Ninth Chords
**9 = Ninth**

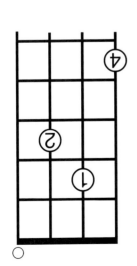

**C9**

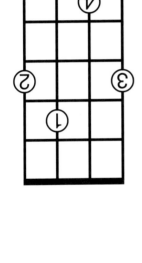

**F9**

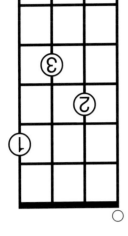

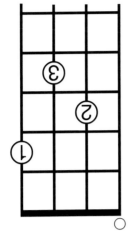

**G9**

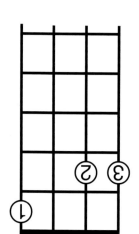

**E9**

**A9**

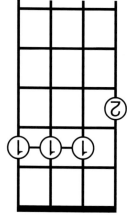

**D9**

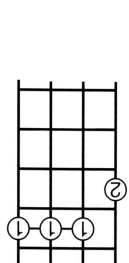

# The Ninth Chords

# The Ninth Chords

**B♭9**

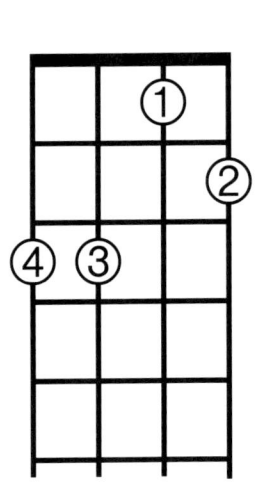

**E♭9**

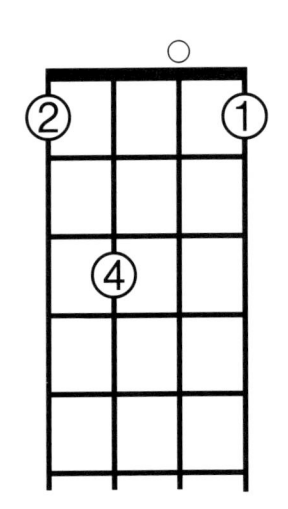

**A♭9**

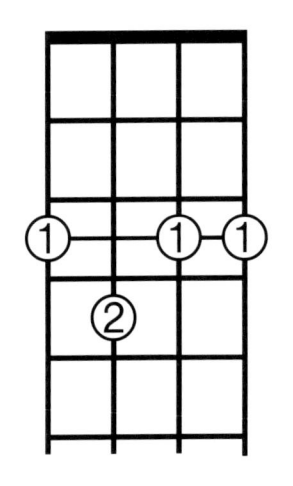

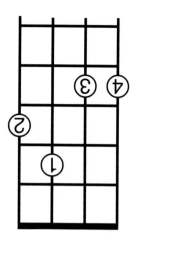

**B9**

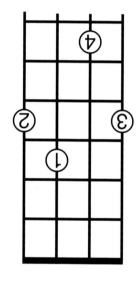

**G♭9 or F♯9**

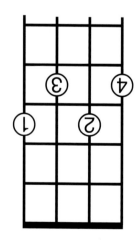

**D♭9**

# The Ninth Chords

# The Major Seventh Chords
## maj7 = Major Seventh

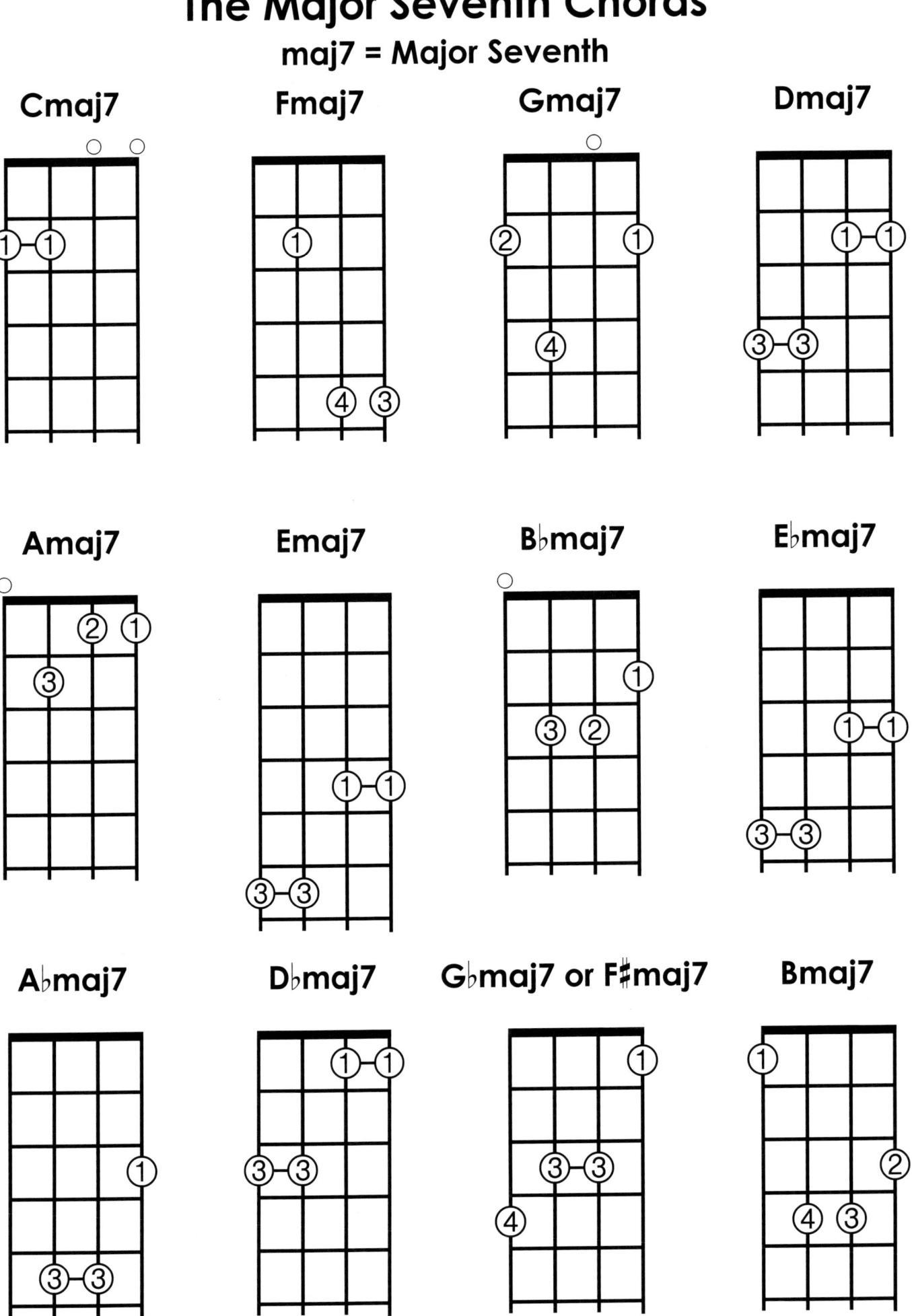

# The Minor Seventh Chords
## m7 = Minor Seventh

### Cm7
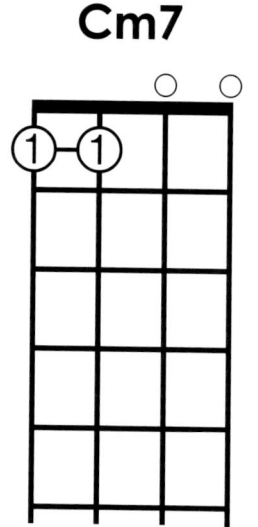

### Fm7
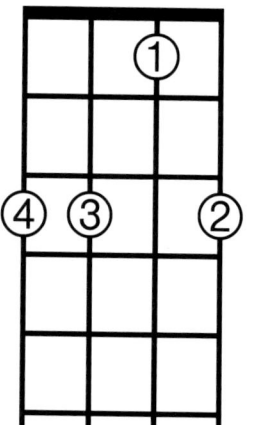

### Gm7
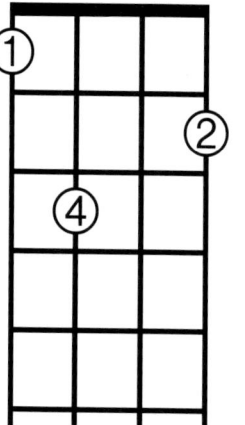

### Dm7
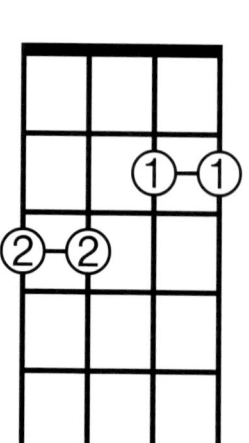

### Am7
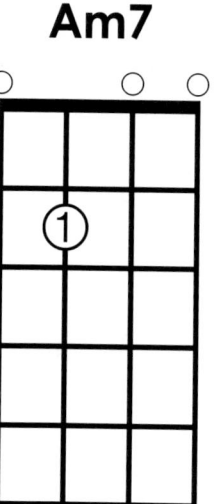

### Em7
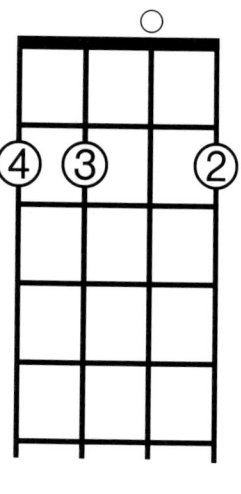

### Bbm7
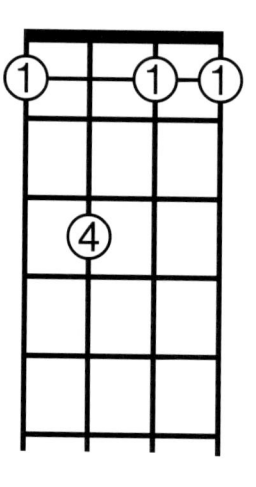

### Ebm7
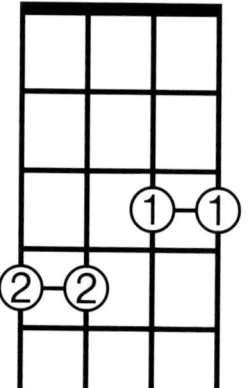

### Abm7
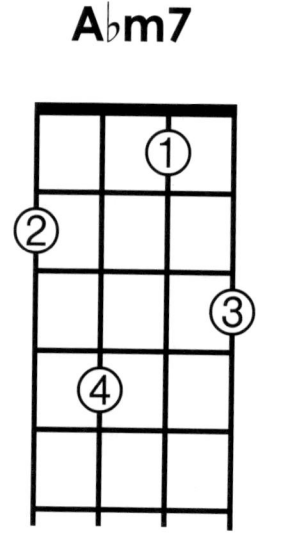

### Dbm7
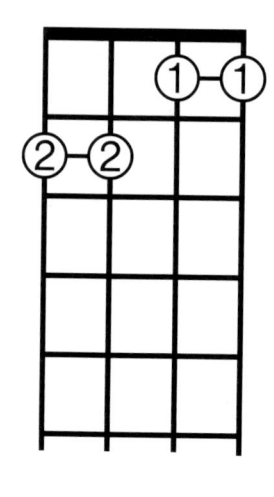

### Gbm7 or F#m7
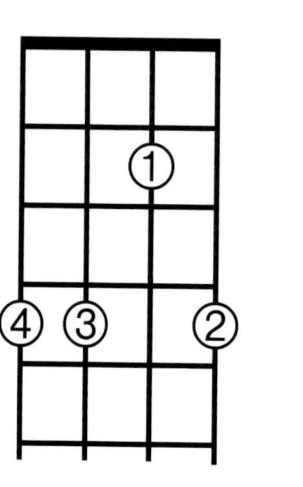

### Bm7
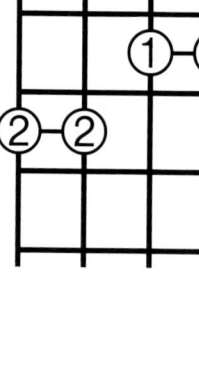

# The Sixth Chords
## 6 = Sixth

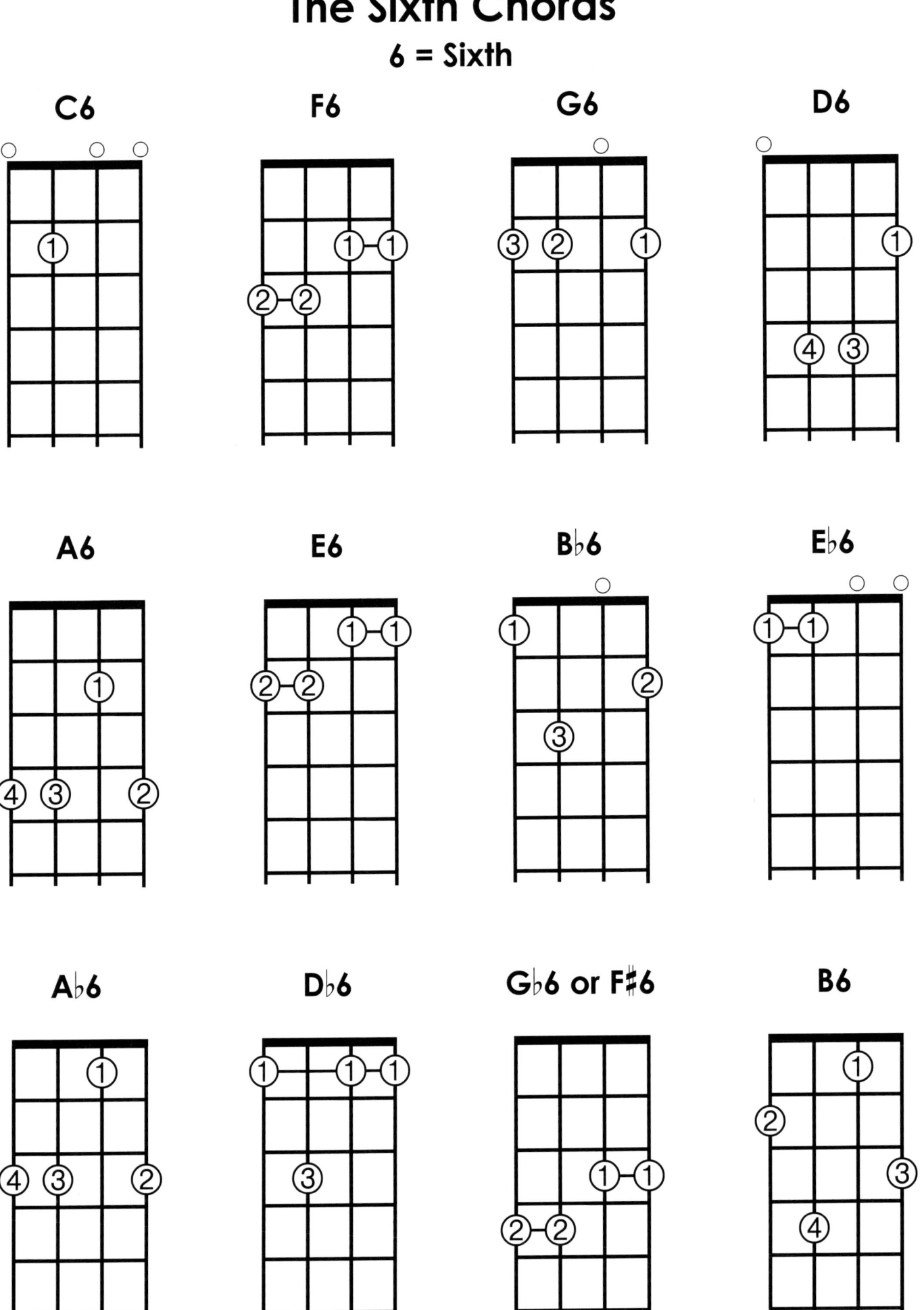

# The Minor Sixth Chords
## m6 = Minor Sixth

### Cm6
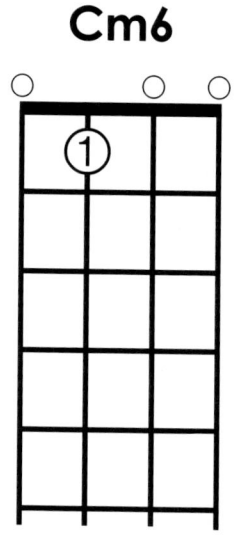

### Fm6
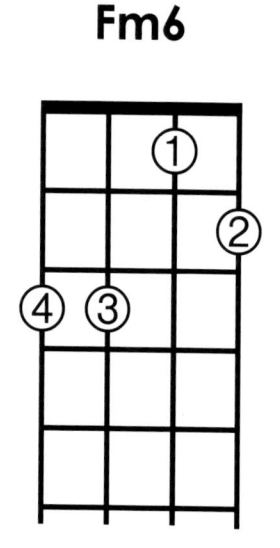

### Gm6
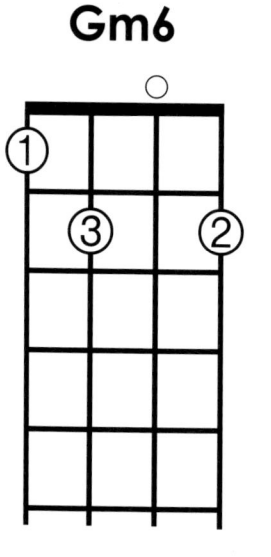

### Dm6
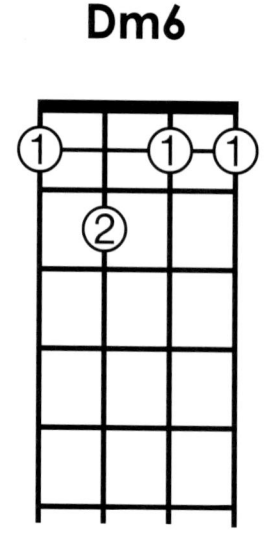

### Am6
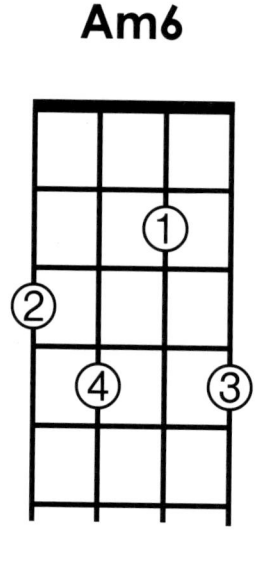

### Em6
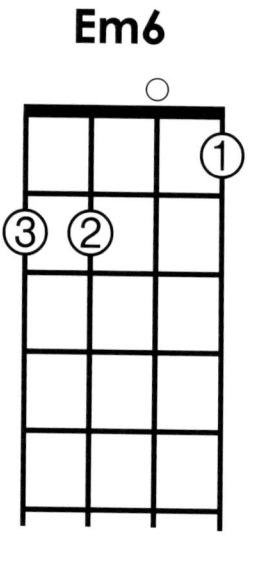

### B♭m6
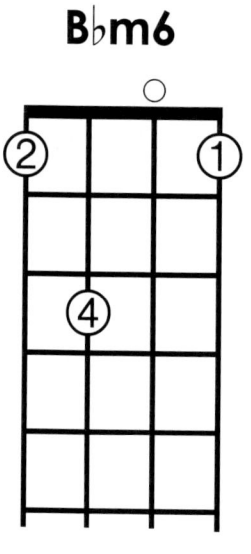

### E♭m6
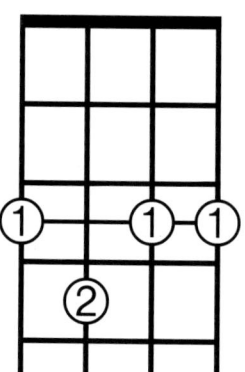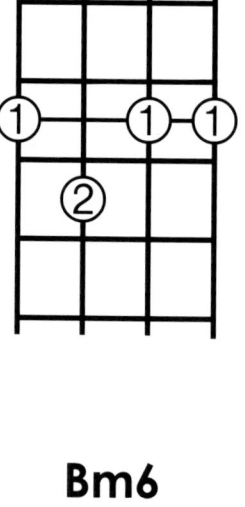

### A♭m6
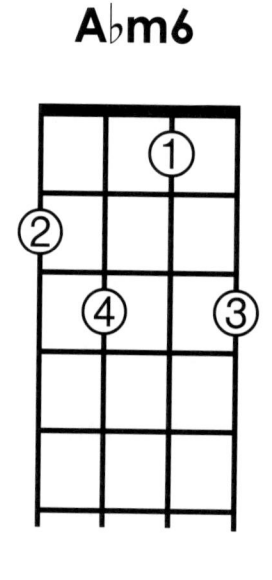

### Dm6
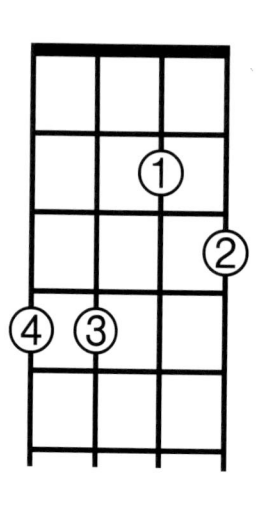

### G♭m6 or F#m6
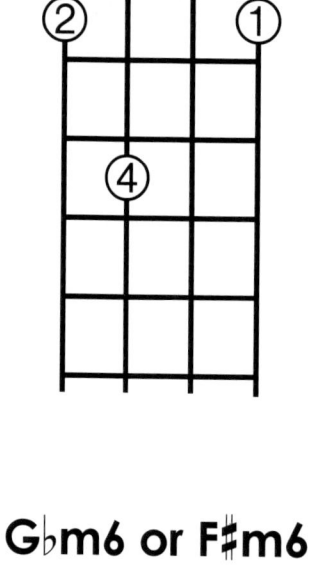

### Bm6
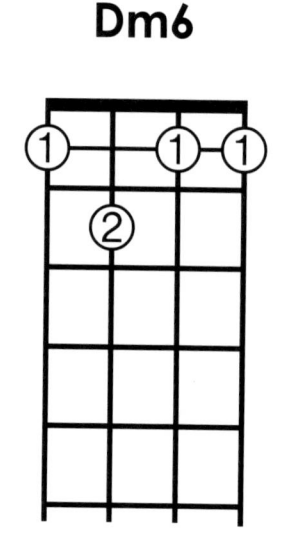

28

# The Seventh Augmented Fifth Chords
## 7+5 = Seventh Augmented Fifth

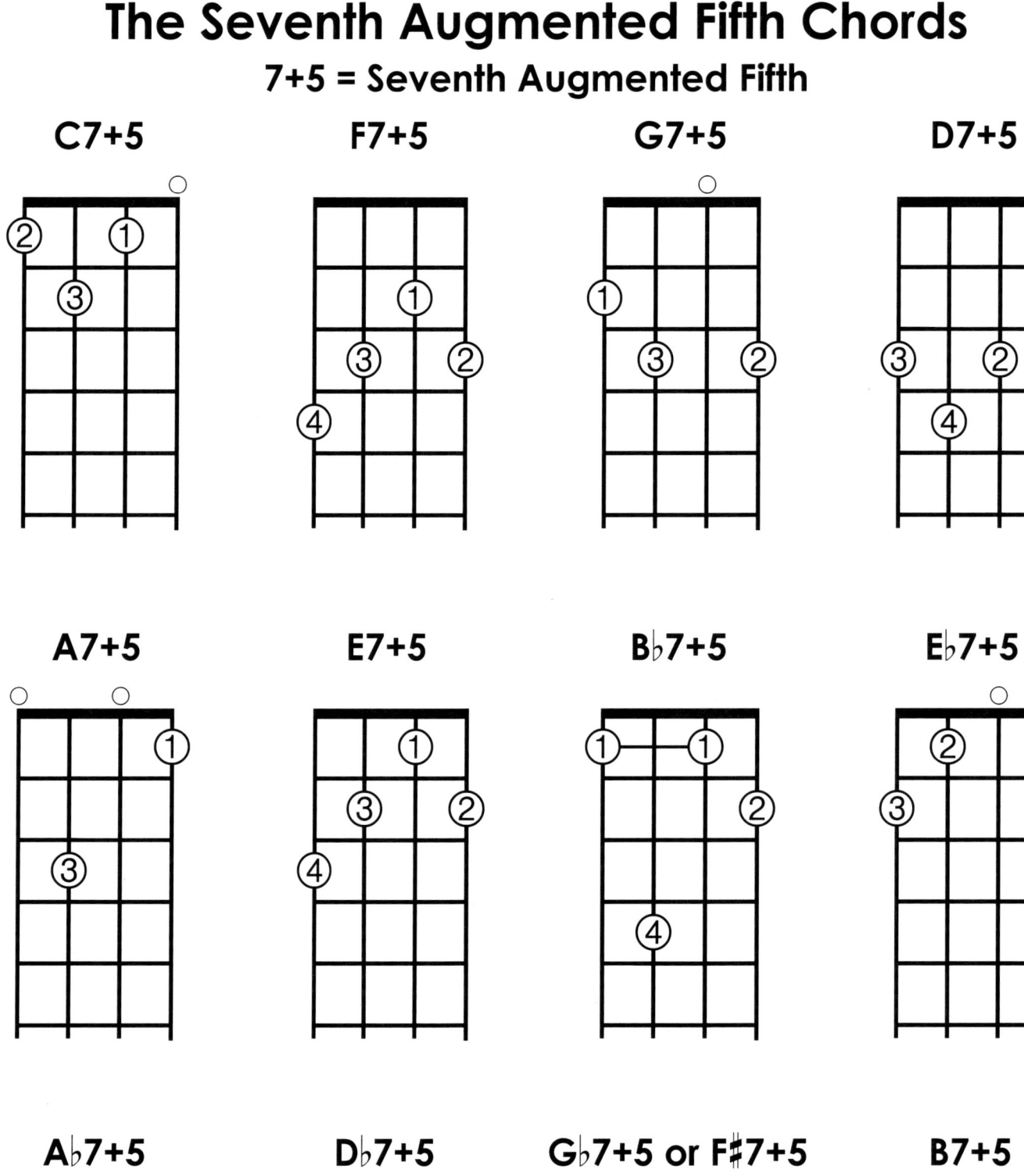

# The Seventh Diminished Fifth Chords
## 7–5 = Seventh Diminished Fifth

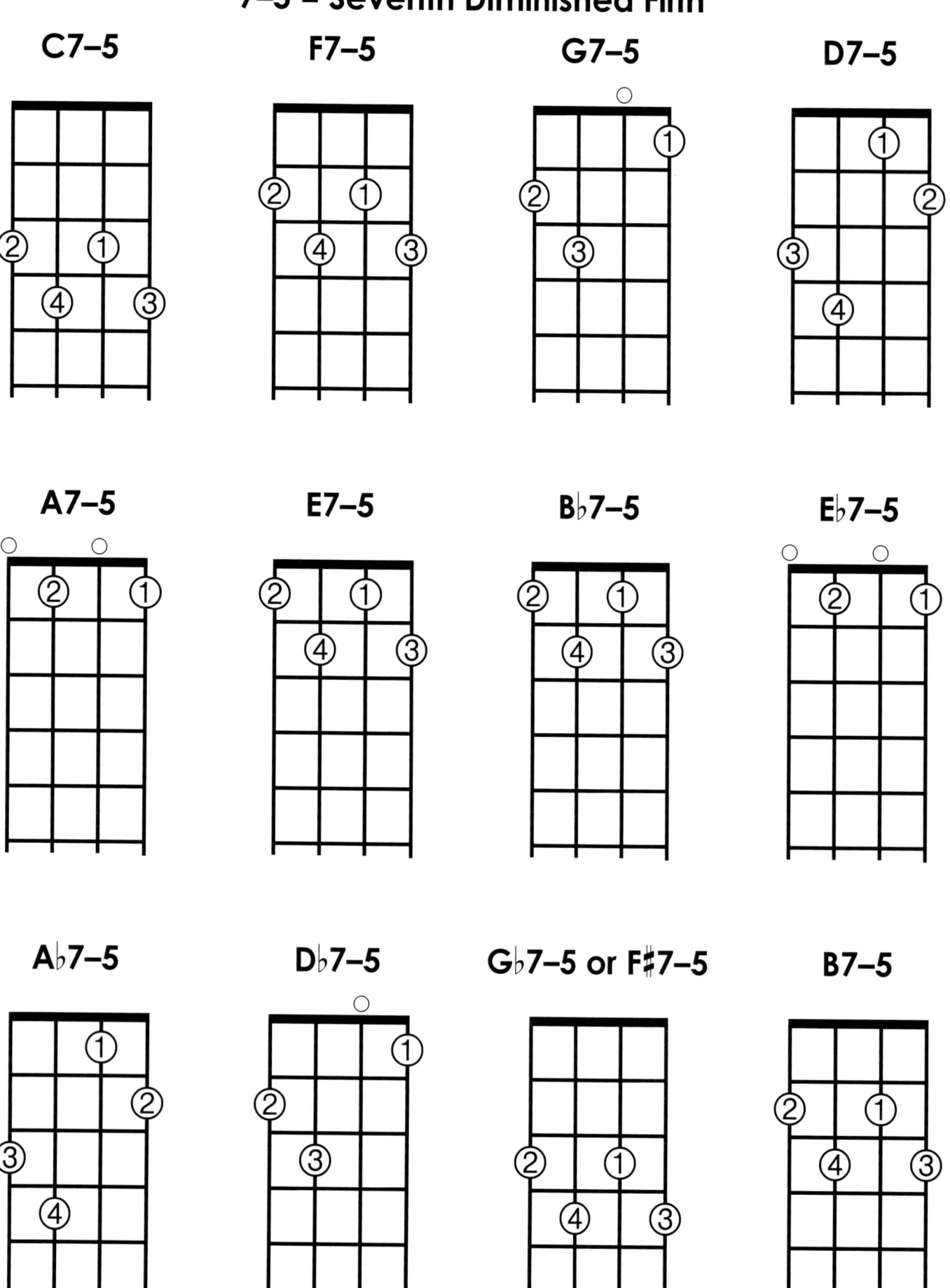

# Summary

The Roman numeral above the form indicates the chordal tone found on the first string.

## The Major Chords

**I**

| Frets | 1 | 2 | 3 | 4 | 5 | 6 | 7 | 8 | 9 | 10 | 11 | 12 |
|---|---|---|---|---|---|---|---|---|---|---|---|---|
| Chords | D♭ | D | E♭ | E | F | F♯ G♭ | G | A♭ | A | B♭ | B | C |

**III**

| Frets | 1 | 2 | 3 | 4 | 5 | 6 | 7 | 8 | 9 | 10 | 11 | 12 |
|---|---|---|---|---|---|---|---|---|---|---|---|---|
| Chords | A | B♭ | B | C | D♭ C♯ | D | E♭ | E | F | G♭ F♯ | G | A♭ |

**V**

| Frets | 1 | 2 | 3 | 4 | 5 | 6 | 7 | 8 | 9 | 10 | 11 | 12 |
|---|---|---|---|---|---|---|---|---|---|---|---|---|
| Chords | G♭ F♯ | G | A♭ | A | B♭ | B | C | D♭ C♯ | D | E♭ | E | F |

## The Minor Chords

**Im**

| Frets | 1 | 2 | 3 | 4 | 5 | 6 | 7 | 8 | 9 | 10 | 11 | 12 |
|---|---|---|---|---|---|---|---|---|---|---|---|---|
| Chords | D♭m | Dm | E♭m | Em | Fm | G♭m F♯m | Gm | A♭m | Am | B♭m | Bm | Cm |

**IIIm**

| Frets | 1 | 2 | 3 | 4 | 5 | 6 | 7 | 8 | 9 | 10 | 11 | 12 |
|---|---|---|---|---|---|---|---|---|---|---|---|---|
| Chords | B♭m | Bm | Cm | D♭m C♯m | Dm | E♭m | Em | Fm | G♭m F♯m | Gm | A♭m | Am |

**Vm**

| Frets | 1 | 2 | 3 | 4 | 5 | 6 | 7 | 8 | 9 | 10 | 11 | 12 |
|---|---|---|---|---|---|---|---|---|---|---|---|---|
| Chords | G♭m F♯m | Gm | A♭m | Am | B♭m | Bm | Cm | D♭m C♯m | Dm | E♭m | Em | Fm |

# The Seventh Chords

## I7

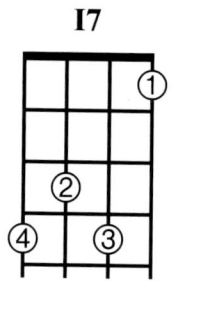

| Frets | 1 | 2 | 3 | 4 | 5 | 6 | 7 | 8 | 9 | 10 | 11 | 12 |
|---|---|---|---|---|---|---|---|---|---|---|---|---|
| Chords | D♭7 | D7 | E♭7 | E7 | F7 | G♭7 F♯7 | G7 | A♭7 | A7 | B♭7 | B7 | C7 |

## III7

| Frets | 1 | 2 | 3 | 4 | 5 | 6 | 7 | 8 | 9 | 10 | 11 | 12 |
|---|---|---|---|---|---|---|---|---|---|---|---|---|
| Chords | A♭7 | A7 | B♭7 | B7 | C7 | D♭7 C♯7 | D7 | E♭7 | E7 | F7 | G♭7 F♯7 | G7 |

## V7

| Frets | 1 | 2 | 3 | 4 | 5 | 6 | 7 | 8 | 9 | 10 | 11 | 12 |
|---|---|---|---|---|---|---|---|---|---|---|---|---|
| Chords | G♭7 F♯7 | G7 | A♭7 | A7 | B♭7 | B7 | C7 | D♭7 C♯7 | D7 | E♭7 | E7 | F7 |

## VII7

| Frets | 1 | 2 | 3 | 4 | 5 | 6 | 7 | 8 | 9 | 10 | 11 | 12 |
|---|---|---|---|---|---|---|---|---|---|---|---|---|
| Chords | D♭7 | D7 | E♭7 | E7 | F7 | G♭7 F♯7 | G7 | A♭7 | A7 | B♭7 | B7 | C7 |